LEO HOROSCOPE 2015

Lisa Lazuli

Lisa Lazuli is the author of the amazon bestseller

HOROSCOPE 2014: ASTROLOGY and NUMEROLOGY HOROSCOPES

ABOUT THE AUTHOR

Lisa Lazuli studied astrology with the Faculty of Astrological Studies in London.

She has practiced since 1999.

Lisa has been a regular guest on BBWM and BBC Shropshire talking about astrology and doing both horoscopes and live readings. She has also made guest appearances on Fox FM, BBC Cambridgeshire, BBC Northamptonshire, BBC Coventry and Warwickshire and US Internet Radio Shows including the Debra Clement Show.

Lisa wrote horoscopes for Asian Woman Magazine.

Now available in eBook and paperback:

TAURUS: Your Day, Your Decan, Your Sign *The most REVEALING book on The Bull yet.* Includes 2015 Predictions.

ARIES HOROSCOPE 2015

TAURUS HOROSCOPE 2015

GEMINI HORSCOPE 2015

CANCER HOROSCOPE 2015

Lisa Lazuli is also the author of

The mystery/thrillers:

A Sealed Fate

Holly Leaves

Next of Sin

<u>As well as:</u>

Delicious, Nutritious Recipes for the Time and Cash Strapped

Paleo Diet: Get Started, Get Motivated, Feel Great.

99 ACE Places to Promote Your Book

Pressure Cooking Reinvented.

Be Wine Savvy

FOREWARD

Dear Reader,

I hope my yearly horoscopes will provide you with some insightful guidance during what is a very tricky time astrologically speaking with the heavy planets i.e. Pluto and Uranus at loggerheads in cardinal signs and Neptune in Pisces calling us all to get in touch with our spiritual side.

I have a conversational style of writing, please excuse any grammatical errors, I write much as I would speak.

As the song goes, "Nobody said it was easy." I know the mass media pump-out shows us plenty about quick fix love, money, fame and success; however, life is a journey filled with challenges and obstacles designed to encourage us to find out what we are made of and who we really are.

Embrace the good and bad and enjoy what is your unique experience.

Be the hero in your own personal life movie and never hide your spotlight.

I must add that the best astrology insights are gained from a unique chart based on your time, date, year and place of birth.

If you would like your natal chart calculated for FREE:

Please click here and fill in your DOB on the contact form:

http://lisalazuli.com/2014/06/30/would-you-like-to-know-where-all-your-planets-are-free-natal-chart/

Please join me on Facebook:

https://www.facebook.com/pages/Lisa-Lazuli-Astrologer/192000594298158?ref=hl

Contents

You are sticking to your guns in 2015; strong and confident in your ideas and opinions, you will not back down and will do your best to convince others that you have the answers. Mentally you are determined and fired up, and this is an ideal year for mental challenges, i.e. if you need to study, prepare important proposals or sell an idea. You can be very convincing and persuasive, and your persistence and mental stubbornness will serve you well.

You can be held back by a certain pride, and you must be aware that sometimes backing away and coming at something from a slightly different angle is not admitting defeat, it is simply being strategic.

Truth and honesty are very important to you this year, and you will be direct and even blunt if it is called for. You will not tolerate people who are not straight with you, in fact, you may even have serious arguments with people who attempt to lie or conceal the truth in some way.

You have excellent managerial and executive powers this year – you are the go-to person for anyone who wants something done and quickly. You are very motivated and will tackle each and every chore or project with enthusiasm, vigor, and organization. Try to not rush everything, trying to complete things too fast or take on too much could place you under more pressure than necessary. Frustration can be a problem this year in many walks of life as you are so impatient and also restless – you need to sit back and think about which situations need speed and which need accuracy and more focus. You may do yourself and your reputation damage by taking the 'fastest is best' approach to every situation, even where it is not the best way.

Leos are leaders. I know there are quiet Leos, who shun the limelight, but you all love to have some authority and some little place where you are in control and can lead. This year that urge to take the reigns and to lead and direct affairs is very strong, and you should go with it.

This is quite a feisty year, where your likes, dislikes and opinions on certain matters are intensified and rather passionate. This can lead to clashes with others, and you are not willing to back down or keep a lid on your feelings. Emotions will run high, and as your emotional attachment to your ideas and projects is intense, this can lead to conflict should you not develop some detachment.

Slow burn anger can be a problem this year – issues that you have repressed or things that you have bottled up may gush to the surface like a volcano erupting causing some unpleasantness. Avoid this by trying to address any feelings of resentment and hostility brewing within you. In cases when you cannot change or rectify an anger issue or bad experience from the past, try to forgive and forget or use a spiritual method of moving on from that negative memory. The challenge for you this year is to address pains of the past and to try and put them to bed, they should not be allowed to taint the present. We cannot always get justice, and we cannot always even get an apology, but we also cannot allow something to destroy us over and over again. Life is too precious to waste.

You are very wilful and determined and will not be easily swayed off any course you choose, despite obstacles. You can be quite vengeful in the moment, hell-bent on not letting anyone get the better of you – try not to let that tendency get out of control. Ask yourself if it really matters that much. You are putting yourself under a lot of pressure this year and are finding it hard to flick the mental cut-out switch as you are thinking all the time; this can mean that you lose perspective and you may act irrationally. Remember to allow yourself time to get away from everything; you must make an effort to really relax and withdraw from the hubbub of your job and daily life.

The first part of 2015 is one of key decisions and critical developments; you will be challenged by various events which are thrown at you, and it will be down to you and your belief and confidence in what you are doing whether you persist or change tack. You may initially react with anger, but this will soon turn into resolve and a problem-busting determination.

Conserving energy is a priority this year, and you must do your best not to scatter or waste energy on lost causes be they people or projects. You must continually assess and address the most pressing issues in your home and work life – anything on the periphery of importance must go.

You will need extra planning and tenacity when dealing with authority figures, the government or employers as they will be exacting and often hard to please – make sure anything you submit can stand up to scrutiny, and avoid the tendency to rush. Do not fight blindly this year, pick your battles and use persistent pressure rather than force or nagging to get your way. Nothing is impossible; however, results in the first part of the year are slow to come and must be slow cooked not microwaved.

Problems you are encountering right now may be directly linked to something you began about seven years ago – you need to think about how your needs may have changed since then and how you may have outgrown this project or how events may have outstripped the project. You must look at ongoing tasks/jobs/aims in your life and make changes that reflect current emotional and financial circumstances.

This is a year of stripping out anything in your life that does not create value, and these can be relationships both social, love and work as well as activities. The things you move away from this year may be attachments linked with your past i.e. moving away from an area linked to your past, cutting ties with certain family members, drifting away from friends linked to a past time and place in your life. There is a strong theme of tying up loose ends and moving on in a positive way.

In business, this is a year of crucial decisions – if you need to cut your losses, do it this year, do not delay. Focus on successful areas of your life and your business and capitalize on these – do not waste resources rescuing failing enterprises and ventures.

This period is a test of both your resolve and your belief in what you are doing – the greater the resolve and belief, the more successfully you will negotiate the hurdles and obstacles. If you feel you cannot push through, maybe it is the universe trying to give you a message that you need a change in direction.

Moderate exercise and low-fat eating are essential this year. Look after your heart health and make sure you get more fresh air and fresh vegetables. You must learn to manage your stress and look at techniques or different lifestyles that can foster better long term health. The sooner you start eating better and getting more physical stimulation, the easier it is to get into good habits which will pay off for a lifetime. This is a great year to break bad habits and start new more healthy regimes in your day-to-day life.

2015 is essentially a creative and exciting year of change and hope – you are hungry for new adventure and have an open mind about the possibilities for your life. Yes, there are some obstacles in the early months of 2015, but with your eyes firmly on the future, you can deal with these with confidence knowing that your appetite for change and growth will bring opportunity.

Activates which can help you to see yourself in a new light and develop a greater awareness of yourself and your talents are very important right now – group activities especially political, spiritual and new age can be helpful and very transformative.

Sudden meetings of new friends or an unexpected new love relationship could allow you to regain an understanding of your true self as if you are actually rediscovering who you are after being lost for a time. Life is full of demands and tribulations; it's easy to lose ourselves and become a collection of worries and expectations – this is a year where you can get reacquainted with you ... the real you.

Within relationships, there is a freedom closeness dilemma this year: one side of you really needs tenderness and closeness and wishes to have emotional support and nurturing while the other side of you needs space, excitement and some freedom.

This dilemma within you can produce some unpredictable and disruptive moments with love relationships. A single Leo may suddenly strike up a new relationship that is unlike the ones you usually get involved in: it may get deep very quickly, but may also be very turbulent and nerve-wracking. The person may be very different in terms of background and beliefs and that may be part of the excitement – he or she may offer something in terms of danger or controversy that adds zest to the relationship and to your life. Again, you may think you are looking for something stable and cozy, but you will attract these roller-coaster relationships as there is this deep need in you to experiment and find freedom in all activities.

Not all new relationships formed now will last, even if the bond that forms is deep; part of the raison d'etre of your new relationships right now is a form of self-expression and self-expansion rather than pure love.

This dilemma will also create waves in settled relationships where you have an opportunity to readjust. All relationships can drift along – we put up with things and let issues slide for the sake of peace. This year is a great time to shake up your relationship – take a risk and address issues you have been bottling up, think about how the relationship can change for the better. Relationships are dynamic, and we often get so insecure within them that we forget this fundamental rule: the relationship between two people is an ever-evolving matrix and changes or fluctuations are both necessary and exhilarating. Use 2015 as a chance to reignite the passion and also to get things either back on track or even onto a better track.

Relationships that are stale and have nowhere left to go may well break up to give you the freedom you need. If you feel you can no longer grow as a person with the partner you are with, then it is time to reassess the relationship seriously.

From August 2015, you will experience a burst of energy and vitality as five planets enter your sign. This is a wonderful time to recuperate if you have been ill or have had health issues. This is a terrific opportunity for new starts, new ventures and a brand new attitude. This is a time to be positive and proactive and to just grab every bull that comes along by the horns. For Leos, who work on jobs where self-expression is key, this is an incredibly productive time when you can suddenly find an outlet and expression for your inner feelings and motivations.

The end of the year is very active, outgoing and social, and your life will be a whirlwind of activity. This is a time serious money can be made in business – you will be lucky if you plan well and have a clear strategy. A very opportune time to change jobs or expand your own business. A career or job change now can mean far more money and benefits. Although this is a lucky time, you are making your own luck! The better you dealt with the challenges of the beginning of 2015, the more successful you can be now. Taking chances and being optimistic while also being cautious is the perfect recipe for success. There is no shortage of motivation and self-confidence, and while you should not allow yourself to be complacent or careless, you can be sure karma is on your side.

Love relationships are excellent come the end of the year – there is a feeling of both love and a renewal of feeling. The great thing about love in 2015 is that it's not stale nor boring, it's sometimes feisty, sometimes turbulent, but the meaning is BACK.

Every time you reach out and embrace a new experience this year, you will be successful. Don't be conservative and do not hold back, or you will miss opportunities to revolutionize your life in a positive yet gentle way. Make changes now that can create more happiness, fulfilment and freedom within your life – do it now!

LIFE

Mercury turns retrograde on the 22nd of Jan, and so it would be wise to complete all negotiations about contracts and other legal issues before then. Discussions within business partnerships and also in situations where you work with your spouse should also happen pre the 22nd as thereafter it will be harder to reach understandings and have constructive conversations.

Attention to detail is very important in January, you must look at fine print and be more pedantic about the finer points. As they say, take care of the pennies, and the pounds look after themselves, that is the motto this month – make sure you know the details, and do not delegate out smaller jobs as the key or solution to a problem may lie in something small you have overlooked rather than something big.

Things within your domestic life will come to a head right now – anything you have not been handling from a leaky roof to a mother-in-law with a health issue will demand your attention. You may have to do a simple reshuffling of priorities or perhaps even a more extensive rearranging of household affairs. Repairs to your home or a family member who has to move in may mean changes not only domestically, but also financially.

Your energy will be somewhat lower at the end of the month – Leos do need the sun, and January in the Northern Hemisphere is tougher for you Leos than for most. Make the most of any sun available and get out in it whenever you can. If need be use a sun lamp and do take lots of Vitamin D and Vitamin C.

LOVE

Issues that arise in love and relationships right now can be related to deep-seated issues from the past that have not been resolved. Rather than projecting these issues onto the current relationship, you are best off taking time to meditate on or even seek counselling to put the former issues to bed. It may be that it is a person from the past or a family member you have not seen for a long while who unearths this issue for you. Whatever you do, do not try and rebury this by going into denial. It may take time, but this is the year for moving on and leaving unhelpful emotional baggage behind.

You are attuned to the deeper aspects of your love relationships right now, but this can be a double-edged sword, i.e. it can lead to deeper understanding, but it can also lead to paranoia. You can sense a change is coming within your intimate relationships, and this is making you nervous. A change is coming as I said in the overview, and it must be embraced not feared as it offers a chance for a better, more fulfilling relationship.

Single Leo are best avoiding relationships with lovers this month – you are not in a place where you will attract what you really need. Strike up friendships with potential mates by all means, but hold back on the romantic side until Feb.

CAREER

Late 2015 is a very exciting and opportune time for a career, and it is now that you want to lay the foundations for that. It can be hard to quit a job: you need to think in advance about how to tie things up, and of course, one must apply for new jobs. So bear in mind where you want to be come September and plan ahead now. In your own business, think carefully about your future plans and make sure that whatever you do now is commensurate with those plans, i.e. do not go into long-term contracts which you may not want to fulfil should things take off in Sept. You do want to put things in place now, i.e.

establishing new contacts which you can pick up later in the year when you make business changes.

This is a very creative month, especially at the end of the month when your ability to be inspired and tap in a mood or trend to create something very current is enhanced. You are not that great with practical things at the end of Jan, but you are very in-tune with people, and so you can make prompt and accurate gut instinct decisions. This is also a good time for lateral thinking and sudden flashes of inspiration that defy logic.

LIFE

Not a month where you will be casual or superficial, your likes and dislikes will be intensely felt and expressed. If you disagree with a plan or course of action being pursued by colleagues, friends or family, you will be very vocal and will do your best to get them around to your way of thinking. I must caution that being too bossy or forceful can alienate others this month. I think you may not realize how strongly you are coming across, and you need to temper your enthusiasm or your opinions a little. In non-conflict situations, you need to back off a tad and be more cooperative and accommodating.

You are in quite a revolutionary mode: wanting and needing to throw away the rule book, this may not go down well and so approach things more diplomatically.

Bearing in mind the above, if you are in a competitive or conflict situation, this is an outstanding month where your feistiness can be used to beat off competition and win battles. If you are in a circumstance where you have to stand up for yourself, your beliefs or principles then you are ideally placed.

It can be a tense month with you not sure whether to go backwards, forwards or sideways – it can be a frustrating stalemate and advice will not be helpful – you are best getting away by yourself and finding your center again. If you do take advice select your advisors with great care and be sure they do not have ulterior motives.

LOVE

You are quick to anger this month and may be bitingly sarcastic – things are really winding you up. The best advice is to walk out on arguments – take a long walk or go to the gym and burn off the anger. Do not say something you will regret, walk away and cool off.

This can be a passionate and sexually exciting month for relationships; if you can direct your energy in a positive sexual way. It is, however, possible that anger, irritability and the desire to have it all your own way can damage understanding and alienate your partner. The best way to keep harmony in relationships is to inject the relationship with some excitement and novelty – do new things together, exercise together or take up a new hobby together. Doing new things that can also enhance your health and social lives is a great way to bring you closer.

Single Leo may meet new potential partners via church, university or travel abroad for business. You could also meet new friends via cultural endeavors aimed at multi-cultural awareness.

CAREER

A very good month for sportspeople, especially those who need to outthink their opponents.

In business and work the challenge is to know where to cut back or where and when to expand. This can be hard due a prevailing sense of uncertainty; you feel the need to act and be decisive, and yet you will find it hard to decide on a course of action. Do not be in a hurry, you should have enough time to come to a decision that you feel you can work and live with. You must take your time as decisions you take now will have a greater than usual effect on the future of your job or business. Do not act rashly with finances, and do not take gambles.

This month is especially profitable for art that is either religious or ethnically and culturally relevant. Promotional activities and trade you undertake abroad must be culturally sensitive and inclusive. Make sure you adhere to Fair Trade policies in your business.

LIFE

The way you approach this month is very much dependent on your age and level of spiritual evolvement. They say only two things are inevitable, taxes and death: but this is not the full story; evolvement is also inescapable even for atheists. We all grow and our attitudes and approach to life matures – some people become more closed and bitter, some become grateful for every experience as an opportunity to grow. How you handle this month is very much reflective of how you are changing and in which direction you are growing. Younger people may see some of the events this month as disappointing and may feel disillusioned and even angry at fate and life. Those who are more mature and take a more philosophical approach will see events this month as a chance to learn valuable lessons about themselves and others. You should see the things that happen this month (no matter whether good or bad) as happening for an important reason – a reason that will benefit you in the longer term.

"We don't always get what we want, but we always get what we need," as the song goes.

Sometimes we do the right thing for the wrong reason – maybe this month, you should not do anything if your heart is not in it, or the results will not be what you expect.

LOVE

Sharing is very important in relationships – in sexual matters there must be genuine give and take. It is not the month to keep secrets or think that you are pulling the wool over your partner's eyes when it comes to either financial or sexual issues. Secrets will tend to backfire. Don't make impulse spends on your motorbike or a fancy dress then hide the credit card bill, it will come out and can damage trust.

Trust and respect of each other's values is vital this month – when trust breaks down, so does intimacy, and the sex becomes robotic and meaningless. There is the opportunity for truly meaningful and deeply transformative sex, but the proviso is that your level of understanding and respect for your partner is more than lip service – actions speak louder than words.

Allocation of the joint resources will be an issue in most partnerships – good communication and restraint are needed. If you want to make savings, lead by example and do not be seen to have double standards.

Leos in new relationships may overlook the great things that are happening as you are so focused on the sex – that is also pretty good. Don't take anything for granted in promising new relationships – reassure and compliment your lover and be generous.

CAREER

Two things are in focus this month to do with money: one is financing. You may have to renegotiate loans or apply for extra financing. You should be successful, and this is a good time to switch loan provider or negotiate a better rate.

If part of your financing involves taking on a partner or going into partnership, make sure you think long and hard about the splits and arrangements and get everything well tied up.

You may decide to invest in a project – this can be a good plan if well researched.

Trust funds and stewardship is another issue – there may be important decisions and responsibilities to do with money you are entrusted with or money that you manage on another's behalf. If you are a stockbroker, accountant, fund or investment manager, be especially prudent and diligent this month.

If you are in charge of petty cash or the treasurer or purser, do be on your guard. Even in jobs where you do not handle money, you may have extra responsibilities with money this month – if you succeed in this role, there can be more financial responsibility and opportunity on the way.

LIFE

Expansive, optimistic and positive – yes, for Leo spring has sprung with a vengeance. You have a surge of energy, and your health will be excellent – we all get a little run down after winter (or even after a long hot summer in Australia or South Africa), but you are now feeling revitalized courtesy of Jupiter turning direct in Leo.

Generous and forgiving, your relations with others are excellent right now, and so this is a really good time to network or start new projects, especially if those projects rely on teamwork, cooperation and require a good spirit. You are very motivating right now – so in any aspect of life, you can inspire others and together create a successful enterprise whatever that happens to be. As you are giving off such a tangible positivity and are vibrant and vivacious, this favours you in all aspects of life where you have to make a positive impression on others.

You have the oomph right now to get the ball rolling on many ideas and plans that were waiting dormant – this period is especially opportune for activities involving promotion, publicity, international trade, publishing and study.

The theme this month is opening doors for yourself by trying something new and creating an opportunity that did not exist before. Opportunities rarely come knocking, but they are not like diamonds, they are far easier to find, and when Jupiter is behind you, it's easier than ever.

LOVE

Your general optimism and fun-loving attitude bode well for starting relationships and for existing love relationships. Eager to let bygones be bygones, you will not dwell on trivialities and will be eager to smooth things over.

Very much with the big picture in mind, you will look to move your relationships forward i.e. if you have been dating for a while you may begin to think of marriage, or moving in together if you have not done that. Married couples may look to renew vows or perhaps add to the family or even take a second honeymoon. Whatever you decide, being stagnant is not an option, you are looking forward and wanting to explore new avenues and new possibilities in the relationship.

Single Leos may begin dating someone who has been in your friendship circle for a while, and who you have suddenly realized is kinda cute. Friendship and shared experiences and goals are very important in all love relationships right now – those who play together, stay together as they say.

If you have experienced some difficulties getting on with your partner and if things feel stale, look to what drew you together, look at the social activities, political interests or dreams you once shared and reignite the interest in those.

CAREER

Planning and promotion are keys to your business this month. As I said previously, April is a fertile one in terms of opportunity, and so go for it.

Leos in employment should seek leaderships roles and display that you are more eager for responsibility – offer to do work for free to help out the boss; volunteer yourself on a busy weekend; get involved with colleagues outside of work; get more involved in out of work team building activities offered by your work. Putting in that extra effort and showing some initiative can go a long way this month. Often it can be hard to get noticed in a large firm, but doing something a little extra that no one else thought of or bothered to do, can get you credit and you will have stood out from the crowd. Leos always excel at standing out, and you guys are very creative: use that sparkle you have and be inventive at your work; go the extra mile and see how that can open doors.

This is a very productive and enjoyable month for Leos in teaching, academia and sports management. As a coach, teacher or mentor you can make a very big impact in terms of life development and confidence of those you teach. You can make a difference.

LIFE

A tricky month with friends. There can be misunderstandings and crossed wires that can cause upset and confusion. It is best to get to the heart of the matter quickly. There is a reason hearsay is not allowed in court – it cannot be trusted. So, do not believe any gossip or stories doing the rounds, get the information direct from the source and then make up your mind. Be as clear as possible in everything you say as not to be miss-quoted.

Friends like any human beings are fickle at times – one should always take that into account. Friends and peers may disappoint this month, but you should see it as a fact of life rather than a personal affront.

Another problem this month is being overtly influenced by your friends and peers – perhaps you need to take a step back and have a think about what they are doing and saying, and whether you really do agree with it. It is easy to be carried away on a wave of peer group popular opinion whatever age we are as the human need to go with the flow is strong – maybe this is the month not to go with the flow. Do not be afraid to be the one to take a stand.

Truth, objectivity and the ability to be rational are really key to this month.

LOVE

You are very loving and caring, and yet you are spreading that care around and so your partner may feel neglected. You cannot be all things to all people at the same time, and emotionally you are feeling quite stretched right now, as if you do not have either the time or the energy to give enough love to everyone.

Communication is the answer, do not neglect to tell your partner that you feel a little pressured right now and will give him/her your full attention as soon as you are able – most people will understand and respond to this.

You may find that a friend is actually able to give you more support than your partner this month, and there is nothing wrong with that. However, your partner may be a little jealous, and so you will have to manage his/her feelings carefully.

Children are also an important factor of your home life this month, and your nurturing and support will be needed by them.

Single Leo will have quite a mixed bag in terms of love – competing partners, mixed signals and sudden make ups and break ups. It can be quite exciting, as long as you expect the unexpected and don't let yourself get too emotionally involved too quickly.

CAREER

Keenly interested in communications, networking and how to use IT to gain an advantage, you are on the hunt for new ideas this month.

A convention or seminar or even a webinar to do with your industry or field of expertise can be very beneficial and can open doors. Use Google+ or hangouts to make sure you are the first to know about new trends within your career field. Remember those 10% who are first to use a new technique or approach, make the money – you have to catch that initial wave before every Tom, Dick and Harry start doing it. So, make sure you read every publication, paper and blogger who knows your subject inside out and react quickly to grab any opportunities.

You may even look abroad, i.e. within other cultures and economics systems to see what folks who do what you do are doing.

If you are unemployed, a friend may be key in helping you find work – they may drop a hint about something going in their office or a tip about what they did to find work.

In your employment, having an open mind and using your insight into social issues can be very important. Take an open, impartial approach to colleagues and be friendly, yet impersonal this month – distance both mentally and socially from colleagues is important.

LIFE

A much better month for decisions. Your perceptive powers are strong, and you can see the parts as well as the bigger picture, which is great for making confident and sound decisions. This is a great time to get your family or perhaps your friends around the table, thrash out differences and come to agreements about how to take things forward.

Good opportunities and good news can come via friends. You may hear from someone you have not heard from in many years.

You are very attractive right now in terms of attitude and personality – use this to win friends and influence people.

Do not neglect correspondence this month – use June to communicate with clients, customers, friends and family members: touch base with people and let them know how you are and that you care. It is very important to nurture and renew all acquaintances periodically be they business, pleasure or family.

This is also a good month to write – maybe you blog or enjoy writing as a hobby. You are very creative and able to write with a fair degree of inspiration right now. If you have not picked up the pen (or rather tapped away at the keyboard) now is the time to start again.

LOVE

Issues of trust and your own feelings of vulnerability come to the fore in relationships. This can be a very romantic time of deep love and spiritual understanding; however, if baser emotions interfere, it can also be a time of emotional confusion, leading to self-doubt and insecurity within the relationship. Your imagination can run riot at this time, and you may imagine things that are not really there – you must bear this in mind. Usually, overtiredness, stress and perceptions from previous relationships can color your judgment about issues within your current love relationship. Whatever you are feeling now, do not overreact to it – wait for clearer signs and signals next month before you draw a conclusion.

Leos often wear their hearts on their sleeves and love grand romantic gestures – this month, you will be inclined to put yourself out there in terms of love, and while this openness can lead to wonderful enjoyment and new romantic opportunities (if you are single), it can leave you open to disappointment ... but hey, life is a gamble, win some, lose some. You should allow yourself the permission to be that loving, giving open-hearted person you naturally tend to be – some great things happen when we let our guard down, take the good with the bad, and go for it.

Compromise in relationships is a key factor, and you should not allow emotional complexes to make you stubborn and closed minded.

CAREER

An excellent time for business decisions, especially if you have a business or service where you work closely with the community and where social issues are vital. This is a very good month for social workers, policemen, and town counselors – you are both sensitive to the needs of others, including the vulnerable, and aware of the larger context.

A very good month for arts management – you are very creative and also able to manage your promotional activities with energy and confidence.

Your ability to direct, organize and motivate will stand you in good stead in all careers, and you can take forward the efforts you made last month. Very diplomatic and also empathetic, you are the person in the office that can be relied upon to smooth over hard feelings, encourage cooperation and bring the team together. Your ability to see problems in advance and make contingency plans is a valuable asset.

A highly persuasive manner along with a keen understanding of the deeper feelings and values at stake can help you get cooperation and win clients.

LIFE

Allocation of time is quite challenging this month: there is a balance to be struck between ongoing tasks and projects and nurturing the new initiative you have going.

The planets indicate new beginnings; however, they also indicate that these new beginnings are not exclusively begging for your time – there are still previous responsibilities that must be honored. So the bottom line is not to forget the old when embracing the new.

You may have recently moved home or be moving home this month – it may not be a clean break, and issues to do with the previous property be it those you rented from or with, or maintenance issues will continue to demand your attention.

At times this month, it is like driving with the brake on – you have to be disciplined and patient, and at the same time you cannot just stop, you must keep moving and keep making bold decisions.

Issues to do with your home life may be a burden. It is possible that responsibilities to do with home and family curtail your freedom to live your own life. It may also be true that attitudes and beliefs of your culture are clashing with your desire for freedom and living your life as you want to. You have the power to deal with these if you are patient and go about it sensibly.

Over-indulgence in sweet and fatty foods is a temptation and must be avoided.

LOVE

An excellent month for communicating feelings of love. You are in the mood for harmony, love and pleasure. Yes, it's holiday season for the Northern Hemisphere and cozy fire time in the Southern hemisphere, and you are in the mood for love. Your love life this month will be one of togetherness, relaxation and romantic walks along the beach. Sex is very fulfilling and meaningful – not wham bam thank you ma'am style.

You are very thoughtful and conciliatory this month – you are laid back and want harmony and peace above all. This attitude is highly conducive to pleasure and openness in the relationship.

You and your partner are very sociable, and this also aids the general feeling of happiness and wellbeing at this time.

Single Leo have an excellent chance to meet a new mate – this is the best month of the year for new relationships. You are receptive and highly attractive. Your Leo flair is in full swing, and you are ready to show the world who you are and what a warm, caring, generous heart you have.

CAREER

You may think that it is out with the old and in with the new, but as mentioned in previous paragraphs, the tried and tested methods and systems should not be thrown out in your haste to embrace change and new techniques. Also, you must not neglect old client bases in favour of a new market.

An excellent month for those who make money writing, especially in the romance, poetry genre; this applies to copywriting, novel writing, promotional writing.

This is a financially opportune month for business involving real estate, mining, farming and consumer products to do with the home. Management of property and issues to do with property or warehouses where you store things may be an issue, so do make sure your security and insurance arrangements are well organized.

Issues to do with financing arrangements and tax affairs are important this month – get some good advice early on in the year to see if a new arrangement of debt or an investment opportunity can save you some tax.

You are very focused at work this month with an eye for detail and the ability to spot things that others do not. You will not have much patience with co-workers who do not pull their weight, and this may be a flashpoint. The end of the month sees a slowing of the pace with more time to chill out.

LIFE

You are exerting a huge amount of energy right now to achieve what you wish for. This is a highly significant month, where the sky is the limit in terms of what you can achieve. You have energy, enthusiasm, eagerness, diplomacy, quick wit, foresight and also the good common sense to be grounded and cautious in what you do.

You must use your personality and your ability to lead – you can inspire others and get them to support you. Use the confidence you feel right now to action plans and start initiatives.

Opportunities right now come with responsibility – that is a moral and also a financial responsibility. For all the flair and fun that is offered, there must also be diligence and hard work to ensure success. Luck comes from hard work, does it not?

You may use this time for a trip of a lifetime – but this trip will have a greater significance for you than usual. You may decide to visit the country your parents came from to get more in touch with their culture or religion – this may change your life view quite dramatically and influence your future choices.

You may also begin either an anthropological or even an architectural study. Perhaps you are volunteering overseas or participating in a charity or aid effort. Your life view is about to expand – it is not just about seeing the world and having a laugh, it is about having your eyes opened and changing your perspectives in a way which you can really use in future.

LOVE

Extremely loyal and quick to react to anything that is a threat or offensive to your family and loved ones, you are taking things very personally this month. Despite your outgoing, fun-loving exterior, you are quite touchy this month and value your privacy. You are drawing a line between on time and off time, and you do not want work interfering with family time.

Love and also friendship is taken very seriously, with you making time to show devotion and commitment to those you love.

Your emotions are quite complicated right now, and there seems to be two yous – a self- confident fun-loving, assertive you and another more vulnerable, sensitive you that only reveals itself behind closed doors or within the safety of your loved one's arms. You are experiencing some barriers to fully letting go in love this month – examine this closely and reflect on why this could be happening. Perhaps you are hurting over something; something you have not fully let go of. It could be very helpful to chat about this to someone who you trust.

CAREER

Pension considerations are vital right now: if you have not started one, you need to think about it, and if you have one, perhaps you need to look at it again and see if it offers value and is worth the money.

There is a desire for the responsibilities that come your way this month, and you are well up to the task, even if you initially feel daunted. This is a good month to act on plans you have laid to change job or career, or even if you had planned to set up on your own.

Principles and being honest and above board are very important to you right now, and you will seek to create a reputation of being just, thorough, diligent and ethical. Ethics is a big theme this month in business, so ensure not only you but everyone around you follows protocol.

You may be the initiator of many staff and team building events, especially those to do with sports.

LIFE

Events in the world outside will have an effect on you this month – "A man is not an island!" Be it politically or economically, changes in wider society will have an impact on how you work and the way you live your life this month. It may even be issues to do with national security. Whether you take an interest in current affairs or not, you should be more aware of news happenings right now and how they can have an impact on yourself or your family. *Be prepared* and *forewarned is forearmed* is the motto – there is no need for paranoia, but the more informed you are, the more you can make informed choices.

Do not rely on others, if you want something of importance done, either do it yourself or keep a close eye on those you employ.

In some cases where Leo are already politically active, you may become very outspoken on an issue of local or national importance and may be instrumental in spreading information or stirring up some action.

You are very passionate this month and will fight for issues you feel strongly about, you are not in the mood to back down or to take anything lying down.

Eager to get to the bottom of things, you will be relentless in getting answers and ferreting out the truth on matters. Cynical and wary of trusting, you will be analyzing and dissecting information, looking for discrepancies and problems.

Be very careful of scams and get rich quick schemes.

LOVE

Issues to do with children will dominate marriages and partnerships this month. Important decisions will have to be made, and there may be an intense clash of wills regarding these. It is a battle between idealism and realism, but the solution is easier than you think and things should resolve themselves by October. Listen to what the children say– do not discount their opinion.

Manipulation, even sexual manipulation and game playing may form part of the relationship dynamic this month. Your partner may make a big deal of some minor issue to get mileage out of it – don't be drawn into this game. Leos are not usually game players, but Leo often attract Scorpios and Aquarians who are rather good at games – whoever you are with, do be more aware of the undercurrents and subtle messages or ploys that your partner or lover may use.

New relationships may become rather complicated, and you may elect to cool things off for a period – this is a really good strategy.

In all relationships, be a dark horse – don't reveal your vulnerabilities, others may take advantage (consciously or subconsciously).

CAREER

An excellent month for investigative journalists and researchers who want to make a point or ensure that a point of view is heard or represented. This can be a powerful time for mass communication – reaching a large audience with important information.

Mentally astute, this is a good month for auditors, detectives and anyone in a line of work where investigation is undertaken. A productive month for researchers and analysts. If you are working on a project requiring intense concentration and an eye for detail, you can be very successful.

As I said in the first paragraph, you need to be politically and economically aware right now as changes in wider politico/socio circles will impact your work life – they may even present opportunities. Ask yourself, is there a new service you can provide to assist people with a new problem or issue that has arisen as a result of these socio/political factors? Is this the right time to change career or job to get in a better position, bearing in mind economic changes?

There may be some financial uncertainty in the markets right now, and so this is not a good time to invest. Be careful to whom you delegate work, and play your cards very close to your chest when it comes to letting the competition know what you are doing.

As an employee, do be careful whom you trust in the workplace.

Artists, writers, musicians and dancers who perform or create works to do with sex, crime, dystopian, mystery, the occult or dark themes can be very successful and creative this month. Powerful messages can be conveyed to the public via art.

LIFE

Travel and the awareness of new information are very important this month. You may travel to do with work or extended family occasions. Something you learn by chance this month could give rise to an exciting new venture – so be observant and be open to your environment.

This is also a month where you must look to use the qualifications you have to either improve work prospects or move to a more suitable position. Are you overqualified for what you do; do you have a love for something you studied and want to use this ability and training more frequently? Leos are creative and must have an outlet where self-expression is allowed – this month, look to how you can match your abilities more closely to a job or even a hobby or some form of community project. Self-confidence for Leo is intrinsically linked to leadership and creativity, and you need some place in your life where these elements, so vital to you, are given an outlet.

Communication is a vital part of this month – turn off the iPhone and focus on one-to-one old-fashioned talk or a telephone call. There is no substitute for quality communication, especially with siblings, aunts, uncles and other people who are close to us – make the time to be together and rediscover bonds with the gadgets turned off.

Ba careful of allergic reactions to both prescription and non-prescription medicines, and do not mix medications. Take alcohol with care and do not get drunk.

LOVE

Self-reliance and self-sufficiency are very important to you right now, and you may actually be a touch aloof in relationships. Do be aware that the way you react right now is strongly influenced by your unconscious and by deeply buried emotions and emotional conditioning.

You can be rather critical and impatient with your loved one at a time when you actually need to be more compassionate. Maybe you are looking at things from your own point of view exclusively, and you may actually be picking up the wrong signals or drawing the wrong conclusions. Be more sensitive, go the extra mile and be tactful – your partner needs you now, more than you think. Maybe you both have a guard up, maybe your love life has become a domino effect of you did this, now I do that. You have the chance to stop those dominoes now and turn your love around. The power is with you: use your ability to communicate to restart good constructive conversation.

Advice from others about relationships is not helpful right now – use logic and be compassionate and sensitive and keep communicating in a kind and honest way.

CAREER

Your ideas are very much in tune with trends and mores in society right now, and they should gain acceptance, and recognition may even come your way – you have the ability to act in time to take advantage of the public mood in terms of products, information or art.

"There is nothing as urgent as an idea whose time has come" – You can provide powerful moral and intellectual leadership, especially in relation to legal work, negotiations and bridge building in conflict situations.

You can be the force in bringing an important new concept, law or system into place. Using your creativity and leadership, you are also able to manage and direct limited resources so that the most effective use can be made of these.

Do not let events you initiate be hijacked by others – maintain as much control as you can.

An excellent month for business related to mechanical fields and also those which rely on maths and accounting.

Shrewd financially, this is a very productive and assertive month for those who run their own business or who are just starting new businesses.

LIFE

An excellent month for teamwork. Leos enjoy teamwork both in business and pleasure and enjoy including friends and family in business ventures and financial plans.

The biggest problem for you this month is the loss of perspective and being carried along on a wave of emotion where you are in danger of going on tangents and forgetting what the core aims are. Misplaced loyalties can also be a distraction – you must pick your battles and not defend those who do not deserve or appreciate it.

This is the perfect month to get your finances organized – clear out the mailbox, do some filing, check your bank statements, etc. Make sure everything is in order and check to see where savings can be made ahead of the holidays in December. A great time to initiate claims i.e. PPI or other insurance or compensation claims if you have been a victim in any way.

This is a very opportune time to seek out secondary income streams – what talents or hobbies do you have that can generate some income.

Leos are eager to please, do not let that create a situation where you overstretch yourself in a desire to impress – you have nothing to prove.

LOVE

A much better and more harmonious month for love, especially after all the confused and mixed emotions of the past two months. The timing in love is perfect, and this bodes well for sex and romantic evenings out. Suddenly, you are both on the same page, and understanding and harmony has returned.

Single Leo are in the right place at the right time to meet someone special – this person may be encountered via work or some financial transaction. There is an element of good karma related to this meeting, almost as if your generosity and kindness in the past has paid off in some way.

There are many social engagements and festive activities this month – while these are a distraction from work, they are doing your love life the world of good, and you are letting your hair down – which is just what you have needed.

You may work with your partner in a literary endeavor.

Writing of love letters or expressing feelings of love via poetry or prose will come easily and naturally.

CAREER

A busy and varied month at work where you will have to multitask and rush from place to place in order to run errands and get things done.

Although you will be time pressured, avoid jumping to conclusions and possibly making a bad judgment – as the Chinese saying goes, "A decision made in haste is a bad one!"

A slip of the tongue or a word said in anger could create an awkward situation – so hold your tongue and think before you speak. The theme of teamwork is continued, and you must be decisive and keep an eye on how everyone in the team is contributing.

This is a very good month for reporters who must work very hard and even be aggressive to get stories and interviews.

Those who work within the machinery of politics, i.e. spin doctors, spokespeople, press officers, will have a very intense month with a lot of responsibility – double check your facts before you put your name to anything.

LIFE

Money and investments are a theme this month. What is important in any walk of life is to not borrow from or lend to friends or family, and if you do manage money on behalf of others, keep what is theirs and yours separate. I would not lend out anything material that you value as you are not likely to get it back; if you are the borrower (which I advise against) make sure you look after the item well as an accident beyond your control could cause it damage.

Hedging your bets and having insurance (travel, card protection, house and contents) is very important right now as with Saturn squaring Neptune you can easily become a victim of an unforeseen circumstance, no matter how well prepared you are.

On this theme, things beyond your control may disrupt the order of your life – this may be extreme weather or a flu virus, and so do not leave yourself with deadlines in December as you cannot rely on the universe to behave.

Although you are working hard this month, you may be a little disappointed in the results, and may also feel undervalued and unappreciated – you should not take this to heart, this is just a passing phase brought on by the planets and must be taken on the chin, do not let it get you down.

I am sorry to sound negative, but I think to be forewarned is never a bad thing.

This is a very psychic time when feelings, hunches and dreams can be prophetic. You may seek out a psychic, palm reader or clairvoyant for an insight into your future or to make contact with a deceased relative – do get a referral and do not pick any charlatan out of the yellow pages. Sudden déjà vu and a strong feeling about a person or a money matter should not be ignored.

LOVE

Children may impede lovemaking this month – so make sure that you have friends or grandparents who are willing to babysit at short notice so that you can enjoy social events and a terrific sex life this month.

Escapism, especially via sex, is part and parcel of December – you are ready to let go and let the barriers down and really enjoy an emotional and physical coming together. But planning is required, December can be hectic with family staying over and deadlines to meet, so plan nights where you can be sure of no bells ringing, phones ringing, babies crying or kids knocking. This is an ideal time for a romantic getaway to renew the relationship bond in peace and tranquility. It may take you a little time to de-stress and switch off, so do not be disheartened if sparks do not fly immediately. A long walk on the beach, a wonderful meal, good wine, a movie/concert and good conversation are the ideal ice breakers. Once you begin to relax, things will flow.

This has been a complicated year in terms of relationships; you have been challenged to take things to a new level and to reach a deeper level of commitment and a more spiritual understanding. No spiritual journey is ever easy – even in love.

Single Leo may start new relationships with a partner who is older, and that relationship will get close very fast, you will find yourself revealing intimate secrets and feelings, and this can be very healing and transformative.

CAREER

Back up data, get everything in writing, and do not rely on verbal agreements. Be as clear as possible in all communications. Ensure tax and VAT receipts are kept in order – take nothing for-granted. It is best to check things over if you have delegated.

Secure your business premises over Christmas.

This is a very good time for arts management and the organizing of theatrical or musical events. This is also highly productive for graphic design, electronic art, music production and art forms like architecture, sculpture and jewelry making. If you work in a creative field which is also highly reliant on practical methods/materials (i.e. pottery) or mathematical (i.e. architecture, musical composition), this is a time of opportunity and productivity.

Those who work with children will have greater responsibilities than usual – you may become emotionally involved and feel a spiritual obligation to step in and help. You may donate to children's charities over Christmas or even do a holiday/Christmas event in the Children's ward of a local hospital or help underprivileged children. If your own children are well off, you may encourage them to collect their unwanted toys to donate to poorer children. You may make many sacrifices this month to ensure your children have the best Christmas ever – Leo love to spoil and make holidays special no matter how much money they have.

BRING ON 2016!

THANK YOU SO MUCH for buying and reading this HOROSCOPE BOOK

Love, light and blessings to you!

CPSIA information can be obtained at www.ICGtesting.com
Printed in the USA
LVOW11s1450120115

422492LV00002B/337/P

9 781502 729231